CHRISTIANE RENNER

A PRACTICAL GUIDE TO THE LENORMAND ORACLE CARDS

LO SCARABEO

A PRACTICAL GUIDE TO THE LENORMAND ORACLE CARDS

Christiane Renner

World copyright text: © 2004 Uitgeverij Schors - Amsterdam NL (www.schors.nl).

Originally published in Dutch under the title 'Trainen met de Waarzegkaarten van Mademoiselle Lenormand'.

Printed in May 2021 - Grafiche Stella

INTRODUCTION
PRACTICING WITH CARD COMBINATIONS

The fortune-telling cards of Mademoiselle Lenormand are among the most used divination cards in Europe, nowadays probably even in the world. The lovely images of the cards immediately capture one's imagination, and because of their intricate design they offer a treasure trove of symbolism and traditional values. As a consequence, the significance of the cards sheds light on numerous situations and offers answers to a variety of questions.

Countless books have been written on the secret backgrounds and the many perspectives the famous Lenormand cards have to offer, but although these books provide a fair description of the cards individually and sometimes even a few card spreads, an explanation of the (inter)relationships between the cards, the so-called 'card combinations', is often unavailable.

A Practical Guide to the Lenormand Oracle Cards is all about these card combinations. Each of the 36 Lenormand cards is combined with the other 35 cards of the deck. That way, the individual significance of each card, when combined with the other cards, becomes instantly visible. Keywords and short quotes describe the significance of the relevant cards in all 36 combinations. All card combinations are shown in a visually attractive and recognizable diagram, showing clearly the combinations by which means the significance of the cards becomes directly and clearly visible.

The connections between the cards offer the opportunity to interpret a card reading more profoundly and in more detail. The complete picture as depicted by the diagrams and the keywords appeal to spontaneous associations of new concepts. These concepts can then be linked to each other, thus creating a perfect interpretation of the cards.

In the back of the book you will find the well-known card spread ***The Big Spread (also known as Le Grand Tableau)***. This spread uses all 36 cards. With the by now acquired knowledge of the card combinations through 'connective thinking', this spread can be interpreted in-depth and in detail.

On the last pages of the book you will find a ***Practice Sheet***, that can be used to quiz yourself on your current knowledge of the meaning of the 36 cards and their connections with the card combinations.

A Practical Guide to the Lenormand Oracle Cards offers a unique practice program, that will bring both the layman as the more advanced card reader profound insight as well as a lot of fun.

However, only practise and experience will ultimately lead to a more extensive interpretation of the keywords and the card combinations. The more practise and experience, the more connections will be made...

1 RIDER

Keywords: news passed by word-of-mouth, messages and communication in general, thoughts

SIGNIFICANCE OF THE CARD COMBINATIONS

2. Clover: good news at last, getting out of a stage of negative thinking

3. Ship: a message or a conversation (in a foreign language) about a journey or money

4. House: conversations at home or about a house

5. Tree: a conversation about illness, news about health

6. Clouds: a blocked communication

7. Snake: discovering lies or spreading them

8. Coffin: bad news, compulsive thoughts, threat

9. Bouquet: news about a gift, establishing peace

10. Scythe: immaturity or verbal insecurity; street or teen slang

11. Whip: a quarrel

12. Birds: unpleasant news gradually changing into relief

13. Child: a spontaneous conversation, talk about kids

14. Fox: a conversation full of schemes, caution!

15. Bear: negative thoughts

16. Stars: good news, good verbal communication skills

17. Stork: news about a change

18. Dog: conversations with a friend

19. Tower: thoughts running in circles, an official conversation

20. Garden: group conversations, networking, speaking in public

21. Mountain: sad news, sorrowful thoughts

22. Way: a conversation along the way or talk about a choice

23. Mice: new information is still missing

24. Heart: a conversation about love

25. Ring: a conversation with the spouse or partner

26. Book: not everything has been said or understood

27. Letter: a decision is announced

28. Man: conversations with the male partner; for a man: someone wants to get in touch with you

29. Woman: conversations with the female partner; for a woman: someone wants to get in touch with you

30. Lily: news from a friend or coach, a conversation about a promotion

31. Sun: positive news, positive thoughts

32. Moon: staff meetings, work related to communication or (a) language, work-related news

33. Key: receiving a solution, a successful or a therapeutic conversation

34. Fish: increase of contacts, constant phone calls, good news

35. Anchor: a declaration of love

36. Cross: news or a conversation about hindrance

2
CLOVER

Keywords: getting out of a difficult situation, the desire creates the basis of the action

SIGNIFICANCE OF THE CARD COMBINATIONS

1. Rider: good news at last, getting out of a stage of negative thinking

3. Ship: improving finances, a desire for money

4. House: an improving personal situation

5. Tree: a sick person is recovering

6. Clouds: the desire to obstruct something, a blockade diminishes

7. Snake: craving to look attractive

8. Coffin: wishing for drastic changes

9. Bouquet: longing for peace and quiet

10. Scythe: a dangerous wish, fear of wishing the right thing

11. Whip: the desire to be assertive

12. Birds: the wish to be taken care of

13. Child: the desire to have children, a child is recovering

14. Fox: making plans, inventing tactics

15. Bear: the desire to outdo others

16. Stars: desiring a new aim in life

17. Stork: the desire to move (change places)

18. Dog: a troubled friendship will be restored

19. Tower: an improvement of the social status

20. Garden: social contacts improve

21. Mountain: sadness decreases

22. Way: making the first move will bring improvement

23. Mice: a shortage or absence (of something) diminishes

24. Heart: creativity will be flowing

25. Ring: a troublesome relation will be restored

26. Book: the urge to unravel secrets

27. Letter: news that brings improvement

28. Man: this man is honest and trustworthy

29. Woman: this woman is honest and trustworthy

30. Lily: a promotion (at work) might be expected

31. Sun: thanks to better understanding great times are approaching

32. Moon: improving working conditions, agreement or (marriage) proposal

33. Key: the fulfilment of a wish becomes a possibility

34. Fish: the desire for more and better

35. Anchor: romantic grievances are solved

36. Cross: improvement is approaching, but slowly...

3
SHIP

Keywords: finance, travelling abroad, the energy flow

SIGNIFICANCE OF THE CARD COMBINATIONS

1. Rider: a message or a conversation (in a foreign language) about a journey or money

2. Clover: improving finances, a desire for money

4. House: money for buying a house (parents)

5. Tree: medical expenses or finances are not in order

6. Clouds: frozen account, a trip is cancelled

7. Snake: lies and deception concerning money

8. Coffin: an inheritance, a source of income becomes exhausted

9. Bouquet: receiving money (an unexpected gift)

10. Scythe: insecurity, immature attitude and danger regarding financial matters

11. Whip: spending a lot of money

12. Birds: a storm in a teacup about money

13. Child: contribution to the education of children, pocket money

14. Fox: a financial trick

15. Bear: jealousy about money

16. Stars: a new financial goal, financial success, a good trip

17. Stork: changeable finances, expenses for moving (to another home)

18. Dog: financial reliability

19. Tower: a financial institute

20. Garden: a prosperous company, spending money on (new) friends or acquaintances

21. Mountain: grief over a financial situation, an unpleasant trip

22. Way: transport costs, money is coming

23. Mice: a shortage of money, theft

24. Heart: an investment in (works of) art

25. Ring: a relationship based on finances

26. Book: school fees, tuition costs, secrecy regarding finances

27. Letter: a message about money, a bank statement

28. Man: a wealthy man, a travelling man, a foreign man

29. Woman: a wealthy woman, a travelling woman, a foreign woman

30. Lily: a raise due to promotion, coaching costs, retirement

31. Sun: an excellent financial situation, travelling to someplace warm

32. Moon: earnings from activities (abroad), working in the tourist industry or with ships

33. Key: solving problems with financial means

34. Fish: a lot of money, foreign currencies, traveling

35. Anchor: love for money and possessions, materialism, a good trip (honeymoon)

36. Cross: financial losses, a financial setback, a trip falls short

4

HOUSE

Keywords: house, private life, father (figure), prosperity

SIGNIFICANCE OF THE CARD COMBINATIONS

1. Rider: conversations at home or about a house

2. Clover: an improving personal situation

3. Ship: money for buying a house (parents)

5. Tree: complications with a house (building)

6. Clouds: a shielded private life, difficulties at home

7. Snake: indoor leakage, faulty gas pipe

8. Coffin: a big renovation of a house or building

9. Bouquet: receiving a gift from the father, a peaceful private life

10. Scythe: peril is threatening the private life

11. Whip: quarrels in the family

12. Birds: misconceptions, temporary sadness within the family

13. Child: the child is at home, an honourable father

14. Fox: there is no openness within the family, just distrust, ruse and deception

15. Bear: a negative father, envy about the living situation

16. Stars: taking successful action regarding housing or buying a house

17. Stork: a move (to another place or house)

18. Dog: a friend comes to visit

19. Tower: loneliness at home, an ambitious father

20. Garden: lots of people around the house, a commune

21. Mountain: sadness within the family, a negative father

22. Way: choices regarding housing, doubts about choosing a house

23. Mice: the house has defects, burglars

24. Heart: a beautiful dwelling, a man in love

25. Ring: a happy marriage in which you feel safe

26. Book: at home not everything is said, secrets regarding a dwelling or a house

27. Letter: a message about a house or from home

28. Man: a protective, paternal man

29. Woman: a caring, domestic woman

30. Lily: a paternal 'protector', getting ahead thanks to the father

31. Sun: a sunny house, a happy father, luck in regard to housing

32. Moon: working at home, real estate

33. Key: advice to stay at home, the personal situation is under control

34. Fish: a big house, a villa or mansion, possibly a hotel

35. Anchor: a safe 'home port'

36. Cross: a house that is too small or sad, an old building in bad shape

5

TREE

Keywords: disease, something wrong

SIGNIFICANCE OF THE CARD COMBINATIONS

1. Rider: news about health, a conversation about illness

2. Clover: a sick person is recovering

3. Ship: medical expenses or finances are not in order

4. House: complications with a house (building)

6. Clouds: a doctor

7. Snake: weak resistance, poisoning

8. Coffin: a dangerous disease

9. Bouquet: returning a gift, a mistakenly chosen gift

10. Scythe: morbid fear, fear to get sick

11. Whip: an inflammation or irritation

12. Birds: a severe illness that passes quickly

13. Child: a childhood disease, a sick child

14. Fox: pathological distrust, pathological lying

15. Bear: pathological envy, being emotionally withdrawn

16. Stars: pursuing the wrong target

17. Stork: an illness with varying symptoms, complaints of gynaecological nature

18. Dog: a sick pet or animal, a sick friend(-ship)

19. Tower: a hospital, health care

20. Garden: an epidemic (the flu)

21. Mountain: being sick with grief, sadness due to an illness

22. Way: the paving or infrastructure is not adequate

23. Mice: illness because of a shortage of nutrients

24. Heart: matters of the heart or an unhealthy infatuation

25. Ring: a troublesome relationship

26. Book: an unknown illness or not anticipating an illness

27. Letter: diagnosis of a disease

28. Man: a sick man

29. Woman: a sick woman

30. Lily: an unjust promotion

31. Sun: an eye disease, insight about a disease

32. Moon: the work situation is awkward, unhealthy work, working in health care, mistakes at work

33. Key: therapy for a disease, advice to take better care of your health

34. Fish: the water management is defunct, wishing too much, an unhealthy view on life in general

35. Anchor: an unhealthy love, clinging to the wrong person or situation

36. Cross: disorders of the bones or teeth, a chronic disease, sclerosis

6
CLOUDS

Keywords: difficulties, a problem, an obstacle

SIGNIFICANCE OF THE CARD COMBINATIONS

1. Rider: a blocked communication

2. Clover: the desire to obstruct something, a blockade diminishes

3. Ship: frozen account, a trip is cancelled

4. House: a shielded private life, difficulties at home

5. Tree: a doctor

7. Snake: an unreliable civil servant, imaginary problems

8. Coffin: dangerous aggression, an obsession, compulsion

9. Bouquet: laziness or apathy due to a blockade

10. Scythe: a great danger

11. Whip: suppressed anger, blocked energy

12. Birds: a problem is quickly solved

13. Child: blocked spontaneity

14. Fox: blocked distrust, problems with a conspirator

15. Bear: jealousy or negativity causing obstruction

16. Stars: problems achieving a goal

17. Stork: continuous problems

18. Dog: problems in a relationship

19. Tower: the authorities or a civil servant

20. Garden: social problems or obstacles in general

21. Mountain: sadness due to a problem

22. Way: a blocked path

23. Mice: a shortage creates a problem

24. Heart: feelings of love are turned down

25. Ring: difficulties in a relationship, blockades

26. Book: hushed-up problems

27. Letter: an unpleasant or refused message

28. Man: a man in trouble

29. Woman: a woman in trouble

30. Lily: problems with a promotion or with aging

31. Sun: gaining insight in a problem, a civil servant is verifying an issue

32. Moon: problems at work, no revenues from work

33. Key: a problem is obstructing progress, but can be solved

34. Fish: believing in difficulties, problems with (believing) religion, no confidence in faith

35. Anchor: a problematic love, refraining from feelings of love

36. Cross: a structural problem

7
SNAKE

Keywords: lying, deceit, cheating, illusions, chaos, confusion, fantasy, dreams

SIGNIFICANCE OF THE CARD COMBINATIONS

1. Rider: discovering lies or spreading them
2. Clover: craving to look attractive
3. Ship: lies and deception concerning money
4. House: indoor leakage, faulty gas pipe
5. Tree: weak resistance, poisoning
6. Clouds: an unreliable civil servant, imaginary problems
8. Coffin: losing an illusion
9. Bouquet: a deceptive gift, misleading peace
10. Scythe: imaginary or unrealistic fears
11. Whip: adoration of heroism, energy loss
12. Birds: brief misunderstanding, deceit leads to sadness
13. Child: a dishonest child
14. Fox: a cunning lie
15. Bear: dishonesty due to envy or negativity
16. Stars: the target is an illusion, intoxication of success
17. Stork: adjustments prevent confrontation

18. Dog: a dishonest friend
19. Tower: an unreliable agency or business
20. Garden: unreliable social contacts
21. Mountain: a rival is spreading lies
22. Way: disorientation, being lost
23. Mice: imaginary failures
24. Heart: infatuation is illusionary
25. Ring: dishonesty in the relationship
26. Book: 'a little white lie...'
27. Letter: fake news, mail is delivered to the wrong address
28. Man: a dishonest man, focused on appearances
29. Woman: a dishonest woman, focused on appearances
30. Lily: an unfair promotion, a dishonest coach
31. Sun: a lie comes to light or an illusion proves to be a disillusion
32. Moon: returning to old (bad) habits, a profession in science (chemistry)
33. Key: pay more attention to your looks, fantasy offers a solution

34. Fish: unfulfilled desires, a materialistic attitude to life
35. Anchor: leaning and relying on illusions
36. Cross: disorders of the bones, toothache, unable to keep business rolling

8
COFFIN

Keywords: termination, transformation, removal, manipulation, force or power

SIGNIFICANCE OF THE CARD COMBINATIONS

1. Rider: bad news, a threat, compulsive thoughts

2. Clover: wishing for drastic changes

3. Ship: an inheritance, a source of income becomes exhausted

4. House: a big renovation of a house or building

5. Tree: a dangerous disease

6. Clouds: dangerous aggression, an obsession, compulsion

7. Snake: losing an illusion

9. Bouquet: extreme tiredness, a smooth transformation process, a dominant mother (in-law)

10. Scythe: panic, intense dread, great danger

11. Whip: severe (bursts of) rage, threatening with violence

12. Birds: a severe sadness that passes quickly

13. Child: a child in a process of change

14. Fox: compulsive mistrust, manipulative deceit

15. Bear: extreme jealousy and possessiveness

16. Stars: operating scrupulously to get what one wants

17. Stork: first period or menopause

18. Dog: compulsive, instinctive action, a manipulating friend

19. Tower: unhealthy ambition, a (too) influential company or agency

20. Garden: radically changing your circle of friends or acquaintances

21. Mountain: bereavement, intense grief

22. Way: facing a crucial choice, having an accident on the way

23. Mice: lack of power

24. Heart: a compulsive or abrupt and unpleasant ending love

25. Ring: an unhappy or compulsive relationship or a relationship that is about to end

26. Book: a taboo, not wanting to face something

27. Letter: a threatening letter, an obituary

28. Man: a powerful man, a man in a process of transformation

29. Woman: a powerful woman, a woman in a process of transformation

30. Lily: a powerful or manipulative patron

31. Sun: possessing great transformative powers, shamanism

32. Moon: work comes to an end, work to do with death, a to heavy workload, reorganisation at work

33. Key: accepting a loss, a successful surgery

34. Fish: forcing your opinion on others, exaggerated sense of self-consciousness, intimidation

35. Anchor: a compulsive love

36. Cross: excessive self-discipline, the end of an era

9

BOUQUET

Keywords:
peace and quiet, passiveness, a gift

SIGNIFICANCE OF THE CARD COMBINATIONS

1. Rider: news about a gift, establishing peace
2. Clover: longing for peace and quiet
3. Ship: receiving money (an unexpected gift)
4. House: receiving a gift from the father, a peaceful private life
5. Tree: returning a gift, a mistakenly chosen gift
6. Clouds: laziness or apathy due to a blockade
7. Snake: a deceptive gift, misleading peace
8. Coffin: extreme tiredness, a dominant mother (in-law), a smooth transformation process
10. Scythe: anxiously avoiding peace and quiet
11. Whip: fighting for peace
12. Birds: free care, difficulties disappear all by themselves
13. Child: a quiet child, toys
14. Fox: remaining in the background, observing
15. Bear: being able to be alone peacefully

16. Stars: a pause, staying focused, a stroke of luck
17. Stork: psychological change
18. Dog: a nice present, friendship
19. Tower: the authorities remain fixed
20. Garden: social contacts outside work or other professional circles
21. Mountain: silent grief, the 'enemy' is taking cover
22. Way: not making choices, a quiet walk
23. Mice: not enough rest or relaxation
24. Heart: a satisfactory, happy time, holiday
25. Ring: a peaceful relationship
26. Book: literature for leisure
27. Letter: a gift by mail
28. Man: a quiet man receives a gift
29. Woman: a quiet woman receives a gift
30. Lily: a promotion, this coach does nothing helpful
31. Sun: being quiet provides perception, a sunny, cheerful holiday, a nice gift
32. Moon: temporarily less work; voluntary work, professional help with stress

33. Key: the solution is... doing nothing
34. Fish: a rise comes naturally, a great gift
35. Anchor: a calm, stable love
36. Cross: forced rest, following the middle way

10
SCYTHE

Keywords: fear, insecurity, danger, temporary break, youthful inexperience

SIGNIFICANCE OF THE CARD COMBINATIONS

1. Rider: immaturity or verbal insecurity; street or teen slang

2. Clover: a dangerous wish, fear of wishing the right thing

3. Ship: insecurity, immature attitude and danger regarding financial matters

4. House: peril is threatening the private life

5. Tree: morbid fear, fear to get sick

6. Clouds: a great danger

7. Snake: imaginary or unrealistic fears

8. Coffin: panic, intense dread, great danger

9. Bouquet: anxiously avoiding peace and quiet

11. Whip: (sexual) insecurity about a relationship

12. Birds: misunderstanding due to insecurity

13. Child: inexperienced naïveté, a fearful child

14. Fox: wearing a deceptive mask out of insecurity

15. Bear: fear and insecurity regarding social contacts and behaviour

16. Stars: fear of the future

17. Stork: fear of change

18. Dog: a temporary pause in a friendship

19. Tower: authorities creating obstacles

20. Garden: dangerous social contacts, insecurity about (your own) social manners

21. Mountain: a dangerous opponent

22. Way: a danger on the road, not daring to walk the abyss

23. Mice: fear of a shortage, a dangerous thief

24. Heart: a budding love will not end happily

25. Ring: a temporary break in a relationship

26. Book: unconscious or unspoken fears

27. Letter: an unpleasant message or a warning by mail

28. Man: an insecure or inexperienced man

29. Woman: an insecure or inexperienced woman

30. Lily: a promotion is at risk, an inexperienced coach

31. Sun: fear comes to light and is overcome, youthful recklessness

32. Moon: a dangerous profession, work is in danger, a student, someone without experience

33. Key: fear or danger can be resolved or eliminated

34. Fish: fear of thinking 'big' about yourself, negative self-image, fears regarding religion or faith

35. Anchor: insecurity about love

36. Cross: misery causes fear and insecurity

11
WHIP

Keywords: disagreement, a fight, quarrel, spirit, strength, energy, competition

SIGNIFICANCE OF THE CARD COMBINATIONS

1. **Rider:** a quarrel
2. **Clover:** the desire to be assertive
3. **Ship:** spending a lot of money
4. **House:** quarrels in the family
5. **Tree:** an inflammation or irritation
6. **Clouds:** suppressed anger, blocked energy
7. **Snake:** adoration of heroism, energy loss
8. **Coffin:** severe (bursts of) rage, threatening with violence
9. **Bouquet:** fighting for peace
10. **Scythe:** (sexual) insecurity about a relationship
12. **Birds:** anger due to a misunderstanding
13. **Child:** an active and energetic child
14. **Fox:** coming up with a ruse or placing a trap
15. **Bear:** anger caused by a negative attitude
16. **Stars:** vigorously pursuing a goal
17. **Stork:** scattering energy, bringing about a change
18. **Dog:** an angry, obstinate friend
19. **Tower:** aggressively trying to move up the ladder, the army

20. **Garden:** working on social contacts
21. **Mountain:** grief causing anger, an aggressive opponent
22. **Way:** being on the road a lot, jogging, exercising, problems on the public road
23. **Mice:** lack of energy, energy leaking away unnoticed
24. **Heart:** sexuality, love
25. **Ring:** a trial of strength within a relationship
26. **Book:** secret plans, secrets of sexual nature
27. **Letter:** an angry letter, a rash decision; e-mail, the internet
28. **Man:** an energetic, assertive or angry man
29. **Woman:** an energetic, assertive or angry woman
30. **Lily:** aspiring to get bigger and better, pursuing a promotion
31. **Sun:** very big ego, great physical strength and virility, self-centeredness
32. **Moon:** quarrels at work, working hard, pulling out all the stops
33. **Key:** the solution is undertaking resolute action

34. **Fish:** great enthusiasm and self-confidence, heroism
35. **Anchor:** a strong sexual, true love
36. **Cross:** limited energy, restrained anger

12
BIRDS

Keywords: brief suffering or sorrow, temporary misunderstandings

SIGNIFICANCE OF THE CARD COMBINATIONS

1. Rider: unpleasant news gradually changing into relief

2. Clover: the wish to be taken care of

3. Ship: a storm in a teacup about money

4. House: misconceptions, temporary sadness within the family

5. Tree: a severe illness that passes quickly

6. Clouds: a problem is quickly solved

7. Snake: brief misunderstanding, deceit leads to sadness

8. Coffin: a severe sadness that passes quickly

9. Bouquet: free care, difficulties disappear all by themselves

10. Scythe: misunderstanding due to insecurity

11. Whip: anger due to a misunderstanding

13. Child: in spite of openness there are (temporary) misunderstandings with a child

14. Fox: an unclear strategy

15. Bear: a short lived phase of negativity and rejection

16. Stars: misunderstanding about the pursued goal

17. Stork: midwife, various difficulties that quickly solve themselves

18. Dog: misunderstanding in a friendship

19. Tower: bad communication with the authorities or a company

20. Garden: social problems that are quickly resolved

21. Mountain: a brief quarrel

22. Way: wrongly believing that there is no choice

23. Mice: a brief suffering due to absence or theft

24. Heart: a heartache will not last for long

25. Ring: a good and stable relationship, temporary problems in a relationship

26. Book: a misunderstanding due to a lack of knowledge or because of holding out on something

27. Letter: a diagnosis based on misunderstandings, an unpleasant message bringing beneficial changes

28. Man: brief suffering for the man

29. Woman: brief suffering for the woman

30. Lily: career problems quickly solve themselves

31. Sun: inspiration, perception, intuition, clairvoyance

32. Moon: a professional nurse, brief difficulties at work

33. Key: resolving a misunderstanding, the need to take care of someone

34. Fish: the concept of life or self-awareness leads to temporary problems

35. Anchor: a brief heartache

36. Cross: structural misunderstandings

13
CHILD

Keywords: a child, youth, spontaneity, integrity and openness, good company

SIGNIFICANCE OF THE CARD COMBINATIONS

1. Rider: a spontaneous conversation, talk about kids
2. Clover: the desire to have children, a child is recovering
3. Ship: a contribution to the education of children, pocket money
4. House: the child is at home, an honourable father
5. Tree: a childhood disease, a sick child
6. Clouds: blocked spontaneity
7. Snake: a dishonest child
8. Coffin: a child in a process of change
9. Bouquet: a quiet child, toys
10. Scythe: inexperienced naïveté, a fearful child
11. Whip: an active and energetic child
12. Birds: in spite of openness there are (temporary) misunderstandings with a child
14. Fox: the child is dishonest
15. Bear: the child is jealous
16. Stars: gaining new insights through a youthful person
17. Stork: a midwife, nanny or kindergarten teacher

18. Dog: a friend is honest and helpful
19. Tower: a children's home, a day-care centre, spontaneity is contained
20. Garden: the child's circle of friends, a youthful audience
21. Mountain: a sad child
22. Way: a choice regarding children, the child is not at home
23. Mice: missing a child, a child is lacking something
24. Heart: a spontaneous infatuation, loving children
25. Ring: an honest and open relationship
26. Book: the child is doing homework, is at school or keeps a secret
27. Letter: mail from a child, exchange of letters regarding a child
28. Man: a man with a child, a frank, spontaneous man
29. Woman: a woman with a child, a frank, spontaneous woman
30. Lily: a child is protected, a wise child
31. Sun: a light-hearted and cheerful child, a happy childhood

32. Moon: working with children at school or in youth care
33. Key: learning from a child, advice to be open and spontaneous
34. Fish: many children, having a naïve outlook on life
35. Anchor: deep love for the child, the child loves you, a spontaneous love
36. Cross: a child is depressed, a setback involving children

14

FOX

Keywords: distrust, manoeuvring, tactics, schemes, gossip, a secret opponent

SIGNIFICANCE OF THE CARD COMBINATIONS

1. Rider: a conversation full of schemes, caution!

2. Clover: making plans, inventing tactics

3. Ship: a financial trick

4. House: there is no openness within the family, just distrust, ruse and deception

5. Tree: pathological distrust, pathological lying

6. Clouds: coming up with a ruse or placing a trap

7. Snake: a cunning lie

8. Coffin: compulsive mistrust, manipulative deceit

9. Bouquet: remaining in the background, observing

10. Scythe: wearing a deceptive mask out of insecurity

11. Whip: coming up with a ruse or placing a trap

12. Birds: an unclear strategy

13. Child: the child is dishonest

15. Bear: jealousy leads to a secret opponent

16. Stars: a new goal is mistrusted

17. Stork: varying tactics

18. Dog: a 'friend' turns out to be an 'enemy', gossip and schemes

19. Tower: the authorities or company turn out to be unreliable

20. Garden: gossiping in social circles

21. Mountain: a secret opponent causes mistrust

22. Way: a choice between multiple tactics

23. Mice: an apparent friend is insincere and is stealing from you

24. Heart: distrust in affairs of the heart

25. Ring: distrust, ruse and deceit in a relationship

26. Book: a secret strategy

27. Letter: this letter is meant to lead you astray

28. Man: a distrusting man, a cunning tactic

29. Woman: a distrusting woman, a cunning tactic

30. Lily: an unreliable coach

31. Sun: an unknown opponent is exposed

32. Moon: distrust, gossip, ruse and deceit at work, corporate espionage

33. Key: advice not to be too trusting

34. Fish: a secret opponent is convincingly spreading gossip

35. Anchor: not being able to trust love as well as the the current relationship

36. Cross: mistrust arises from frustration and insecurity

15
BEAR

Keywords: jealousy, envy, dissatisfaction, irritation, negativity

SIGNIFICANCE OF THE CARD COMBINATIONS

1. **Rider:** negative thoughts
2. **Clover:** the desire to outdo others
3. **Ship:** jealousy about money
4. **House:** a negative father, envy about the living situation
5. **Tree:** pathological envy, being emotionally withdrawn
6. **Clouds:** jealousy or negativity causing obstruction
7. **Snake:** dishonesty due to envy or negativity
8. **Coffin:** being extremely jealous and possessive
9. **Bouquet:** being able to be alone peacefully
10. **Scythe:** fear and insecurity regarding social contacts and behaviour
11. **Whip:** anger caused by a negative attitude
12. **Birds:** a short lived phase of negativity and rejection
13. **Child:** the child is jealous
14. **Fox:** a secret opponent is jealous
16. **Stars:** not granting yourself or others success

17. **Stork:** discord causes a transformation
18. **Dog:** a friend is dissatisfied or jealous
19. **Tower:** dissatisfaction within a company or with the authorities
20. **Garden:** within a group there is a lot of mutual unease
21. **Mountain:** an envious opponent
22. **Way:** a disagreement leads to seeking alternative solutions
23. **Mice:** discord and irritation due to a shortage of things
24. **Heart:** jealousy and love go hand in hand
25. **Ring:** discord and irritation within a relationship
26. **Book:** unspoken unease and irritation, an unsatisfying education
27. **Letter:** a decision made out of discord and irritation
28. **Man:** a dissatisfied or jealous man
29. **Woman:** a dissatisfied or jealous woman
30. **Lily:** dissatisfactory guidance, displeasure with a career

31. **Sun:** not granting yourself or others a good reputation, not being allowed to be yourself
32. **Moon:** envy, irritations and dissatisfaction at the workplace
33. **Key:** the advice to become aware of your own irritations and unease
34. **Fish:** discord due to a negative approach on life in general
35. **Anchor:** in this relationship is a lot of jealousy
36. **Cross:** irritation and unease originate from self-imposed restrictions

16
STARS

Keywords: sense of purpose, (strive for) success, a new beginning

SIGNIFICANCE OF THE CARD COMBINATIONS

1. Rider: good news, good verbal communication skills

2. Clover: desiring a new aim in life

3. Ship: a new financial goal, financial success, a good trip

4. House: taking successful action regarding housing or buying a house

5. Tree: pursuing the wrong target

6. Clouds: problems achieving a goal

7. Snake: the target is an illusion, intoxication of success

8. Coffin: operating scrupulously to get what one wants

9. Bouquet: a pause, staying focused, a stroke of luck

10. Scythe: fear of the future

11. Whip: vigorously pursuing a goal

12. Birds: misunderstanding about the pursued goal

13. Child: gaining new insights through a youthful person

14. Fox: a new goal is mistrusted

15. Bear: not granting yourself or others success

17. Stork: bringing about a beneficial change

18. Dog: a strong-willed friend

19. Tower: achieving success regarding a business

20. Garden: a group of successful or purposeful people

21. Mountain: being purposefully and successfully waylaid by a competitor or rival

22. Way: having two strings to his bow, doubting the aim

23. Mice: there is no target

24. Heart: a new infatuation

25. Ring: a successful or new partnership

26. Book: a purposeful study, research yield results

27. Letter: very good news by mail, a promising decision

28. Man: a strong-willed, successful man

29. Woman: a strong-willed, successful woman

30. Lily: a promotion, purposeful guidance

31. Sun: unexpected success, having a clear target in mind

32. Moon: success or a new promising goal at the work place

33. Key: the advice to act purposefully and determined creates success

34. Fish: a huge success, but also: too much willpower and excessive self-awareness

35. Anchor: a new love comes into view, a good cause

36. Cross: keep calm, don't skip one step on the stairs to success

17
STORK

Keywords: change, moving house, variability, relocation, flexibility

SIGNIFICANCE OF THE CARD COMBINATIONS

1. Rider: news about a change
2. Clover: the desire to move (change places)
3. Ship: changeable finances, expenses for moving (to another home)
4. House: a move (to another place or house)
5. Tree: an illness with varying symptoms, complaints of gynaecological nature
6. Clouds: consecutive problems
7. Snake: adjustments prevent confrontation
8. Coffin: first period or menopause
9. Bouquet: psychological change
10. Scythe: fear of change
11. Whip: scattering energy, bringing about a change
12. Birds: various difficulties that quickly solve themselves, midwife
13. Child: a midwife, nanny or kindergarten teacher
14. Fox: varying tactics
15. Bear: discord causes a transformation
16. Stars: bringing about a beneficial change

18. Dog: fluctuating friendships
19. Tower: a moving company, a business is going to move
20. Garden: a changing circle of friends and acquaintances
21. Mountain: a rival or competitor knows how to adjust to the (new) situation
22. Way: indecisiveness, constantly setting new aims
23. Mice: lacking flexibility
24. Heart: feelings of love are subject to change
25. Ring: a change within a relationship or partnership
26. Book: keeping a change obscured
27. Letter: a vague decision, keeping all options open
28. Man: a man who constantly changes plans or aims, a man in an alternating situation
29. Woman: a woman who constantly changes plans or goals, a woman in a changeable situation
30. Lily: a change of career, help when making a change

31. Sun: a beneficial change
32. Moon: changes at work, a flexible job, a job agency
33. Key: the advice to adjust or to make a change
34. Fish: confidently following the 'flow of life', a change for the better
35. Anchor: the romance still exists, but is subject to heavy fluctuations
36. Cross: a change comes with adversity and delay

18 DOG

Keywords: friendship, helpfulness, loyalty and reliability

SIGNIFICANCE OF THE CARD COMBINATIONS

1. Rider: conversations with a friend

2. Clover: a troubled friendship will be restored

3. Ship: financial reliability

4. House: a friend comes to visit

5. Tree: a sick pet or animal, a sick friend (ship)

6. Clouds: problems in a relationship

7. Snake: a dishonest friend

8. Coffin: compulsive, instinctive action, a manipulating friend

9. Bouquet: a nice present, friendship

10. Scythe: a temporary pause in a friendship

11. Whip: an angry, obstinate friend

12. Birds: misunderstanding in a friendship

13. Child: a friend is honest and helpful

14. Fox: a 'friend' turns out to be an 'enemy', gossip and schemes

15. Bear: a friend is dissatisfied or jealous

16. Stars: a strong-willed friend

17. Stork: fluctuating friendships

19. Tower: friendly professional relationships, the authorities are helpful

20. Garden: bosom friends, a large and close circle of friends

21. Mountain: a friend is brooding or is sad, sadness due to a friendship

22. Way: visiting a friend, making choices in a friendship

23. Mice: losing a friendship or rather picking up a friendship

24. Heart: a deep infatuation, a friend is an artist

25. Ring: a reliable relationship

26. Book: a college friend, a friend with a secret or a secret friendship

27. Letter: mail from a friend

28. Man: this man is standing by his friend's side

29. Woman: this woman is standing by her friend's side

30. Lily: this 'patron' is also a reliable friend

31. Sun: lasting happiness, a happy and inspiring friendship

32. Moon: a reliable employee, friendship at work, working with animals

33. Key: the advice to spend more time with friends, a friend provides the solution

34. Fish: having a large circle of friends, friends with the same vision

35. Anchor: a loyal romance

36. Cross: (care giving) obligations towards friends

19
TOWER

Keywords: the authorities, a large company or building, ambition, top job, loneliness, arrogance

SIGNIFICANCE OF THE CARD COMBINATIONS

1. Rider: thoughts running in circles, an official conversation

2. Clover: an improvement of the social status

3. Ship: a financial institute

4. House: loneliness at home, an ambitious father

5. Tree: a hospital, health care

6. Clouds: the authorities or a civil servant

7. Snake: an unreliable agency or business

8. Coffin: unhealthy ambition, a (too) influential company or agency

9. Bouquet: the authorities remain fixed

10. Scythe: authorities creating obstacles

11. Whip: aggressively trying to move up the ladder, the army

12. Birds: bad communication with the authorities or a company

13. Child: a children's home, a day-care centre, spontaneity is contained

14. Fox: the authorities or company turn out to be unreliable

15. Bear: dissatisfaction within a company or with the authorities

16. Stars: achieving success regarding a business

17. Stork: a moving company, a business is going to move

18. Dog: friendly professional relationships, the authorities are helpful

20. Garden: members of a cultural club, study, society or club

21. Mountain: fruitless brooding about life and career, the authorities are not helpful

22. Way: crossroads in life, a transport company, a road construction

23. Mice: a lack of protection, theft by the authorities or by a company

24. Heart: building a wall, not allowing or not showing feelings of love

25. Ring: an emotionally distant relationship, an official relationship, a corporate merger

26. Book: an educational or research institute, a publishing company, an (academic) education

27. Letter: an official letter or document

28. Man: this man is hiding behind a self-built imaginary wall

29. Woman: a woman is hiding behind a self-built imaginary wall

30. Lily: having a so-called high placed benefactor

31. Sun: being able to perceive 'dividing walls', screening a business

32. Moon: ambition, a job high up, making a career for yourself

33. Key: a separation or divorce

34. Fish: expressing an official point of view, a multinational, the ministry

35. Anchor: not yielding to true love, giving all attention to a professional life

36. Cross: a hard time for business, obligations towards the authorities

20
GARDEN

Keywords: social contacts, (large) groups of people, public

SIGNIFICANCE OF THE CARD COMBINATIONS

1. Rider: group conversations, networking, speaking in public

2. Clover: social contacts improve

3. Ship: a prosperous company, spending money on (new) friends or acquaintances

4. House: lots of people around the house, a commune

5. Tree: an epidemic (the flu)

6. Clouds: social problems or obstacles in general

7. Snake: unreliable social contacts

8. Coffin: radically changing your circle of friends or acquaintances

9. Bouquet: social contacts outside work or other professional circles

10. Scythe: dangerous social contacts, insecurity about (your own) social manners

11. Whip: working on social contacts

12. Birds: social problems that are quickly resolved

13. Child: the child's circle of friends, a youthful audience

14. Fox: gossiping in social circles

15. Bear: within a group there is a lot of mutual unease

16. Stars: a group of successful or purposeful people

17. Stork: a changing circle of friends and acquaintances

18. Dog: bosom friends, a large and close circle of friends

19. Tower: members of a cultural club, study, society or club

21. Mountain: animosity or sorrow within the circle of friends, brooding about friendships

22. Way: going out with a group, facing a decision regarding (new) social contacts

23. Mice: losing friends or acquaintances, losing his 'audience'

24. Heart: artistic circles, tolerant friends, falling in love with a friend

25. Ring: a good partnership, collaboration, a close and harmonious marriage

26. Book: friendly and helpful study partners, a secret society

27. Letter: exchanging messages with friends

28. Man: this man has a large circle of friends and is very sociable

29. Woman: this woman has a large circle of friends and is very sociable

30. Lily: moving up the ladder through networking, having the support of a good friend

31. Sun: a happy time with social contacts, insights on the social front, popularity

32. Moon: working (together) with people, clubs and societies, 'networking', a public appearance

33. Key: give more attention to social contacts, a circle of acquaintances provides solution, group therapy

34. Fish: expansion of a circle of friends and acquaintances

35. Anchor: loving each other deeply and enjoying spending time in each other's presence

36. Cross: the circle of friends and acquaintances is getting smaller

21
MOUNTAIN

Keywords: sadness, brooding, animosity

SIGNIFICANCE OF THE CARD COMBINATIONS

1. Rider: sad news, sorrowful thoughts

2. Clover: sadness decreases

3. Ship: grief over a financial situation, an unpleasant trip

4. House: sadness within the family, a negative father

5. Tree: being sick with grief, sadness due to an illness

6. Clouds: sadness due to a problem

7. Snake: a rival is spreading lies

8. Coffin: bereavement, intense grief

9. Bouquet: silent grief, the 'enemy' is taking cover

10. Scythe: a dangerous opponent

11. Whip: grief causes anger, an aggressive opponent

12. Birds: a brief quarrel

13. Child: a sad child

14. Fox: a secret opponent causes grief

15. Bear: an envious opponent

16. Stars: being purposefully and successfully waylaid by a competitor or rival

17. Stork: a rival or competitor knows how to adjust to the (new) situation

18. Dog: a friend is brooding or is sad, sadness due to a friendship

19. Tower: fruitless brooding about life and career, the authorities are not helpful

20. Garden: animosity or sorrow within the circle of friends, brooding about friendships

22. Way: facing an unpleasant choice, hostile behaviour on the street

23. Mice: someone who wishes you harm turns out to be a thief, grief over a loss

24. Heart: heartbreak

25. Ring: grief over a relationship

26. Book: learning problems, problems at school, an educational institution is not helpful

27. Letter: a letter containing an unpleasant message, a sad decision

28. Man: a sad, brooding or negative man

29. Woman: a sad, brooding or negative woman

30. Lily: career problems, struggling with ageing

31. Sun: unexpected opposition, an unexpected opponent, mood-swings, a silver lining

32. Moon: competition and contradictions at work, worrying about work

33. Key: recognising one's own grief, protect yourself against other people's quarrels

34. Fish: frustrated ambitions, meeting a lot of resistance

35. Anchor: a painful heartbreak over a true love

36. Cross: long lasting or suppressed grief

22
WAY

Keywords: a choice, doubt, being on the road

SIGNIFICANCE OF THE CARD COMBINATIONS

1. Rider: a conversation along the way or talk about a choice

2. Clover: making the first move will bring improvement

3. Ship: transport costs, money is coming

4. House: choices regarding housing, doubts about choosing a house

5. Tree: the paving or infrastructure is not adequate

6. Clouds: a blocked path

7. Snake: disorientation, being lost

8. Coffin: facing a crucial choice, having an accident on the way

9. Bouquet: not making a choice, a quiet walk

10. Scythe: a danger on the road, not daring to walk the abyss

11. Whip: being on the road a lot, jogging, exercising, problems on the public road

12. Birds: wrongly believing that there is no choice

13. Child: a choice regarding children, the child is not at home

14. Fox: a choice between multiple tactics

15. Bear: a disagreement leads to seeking alternative solutions

16. Stars: having two strings to his bow, doubting the aim

17. Stork: indecisiveness, constantly setting new aims

18. Dog: visiting a friend, making choices in a friendship

19. Tower: crossroads in life, a transport company, a road construction

20. Garden: going out with a group, facing a decision regarding (new) social contacts

21. Mountain: facing an unpleasant choice, hostile behaviour on the street

23. Mice: pickpockets or other smalltimers, regrets about a material issue

24. Heart: a choice from the heart, regrets about a metaphysical issue, doubts about a work of art

25. Ring: facing a choice regarding a relationship

26. Book: not being able to choose regarding a school or education, doubting the aim

27. Letter: a message is already on the way, a message involves a choice

28. Man: this man is having second thoughts and finds it hard to choose, he is on the road a lot

29. Woman: this woman is having second thoughts and finds it hard to choose, she is on the road a lot

30. Lily: a choice to get a promotion, the coach's choice

31. Sun: an outing with lovely weather, a clear choice, tolerance in traffic

32. Moon: a choice regarding work or profession, road works, working outside, transport industry

33. Key: postponing a decision in order to investigate its possibilities and consequences

34. Fish: waterways, having a lot of options, a generous offer

35. Anchor: a true love necessitates an important choice

36. Cross: a new phase of life entails limited options

23

MICE

Keywords:
theft, shortage, absence, missing (someone)

SIGNIFICANCE OF THE CARD COMBINATIONS

1. Rider: new information is still missing

2. Clover: a shortage or absence (of something) diminishes

3. Ship: a shortage of money, theft

4. House: the house has defects, burglars

5. Tree: illness because of a shortage of nutrients

6. Clouds: a shortage creates a problem

7. Snake: imaginary failures

8. Coffin: lack of power

9. Bouquet: not enough rest or relaxation

10. Scythe: fear of a shortage, a dangerous thief

11. Whip: lack of energy, energy leaking away unnoticed

12. Birds: a brief suffering due to absence or theft

13. Child: missing a child, a child is lacking something

14. Fox: an apparent friend is insincere and is stealing from you

15. Bear: discord and irritation due to a shortage of things

16. Stars: there is no target

17. Stork: lacking flexibility

18. Dog: losing a friendship or rather picking up a friendship

19. Tower: a lack of protection, theft by the authorities or by a company

20. Garden: losing friends or acquaintances, losing his 'audience'

21. Mountain: someone who wishes you harm turns out to be a thief, grief over a loss

22. Way: pickpockets or other small-timer's, regrets about a material issue

24. Heart: losing a loved one, missing love

25. Ring: missing a relationship, a diminishing relationship

26. Book: a lack of education or knowledge, an educational institution falls short, an undiscovered or unexplained theft

27. Letter: a letter gets lost, lost papers, message about a theft

28. Man: a man with shortcomings, a person or object that was presumed lost shows up again

29. Woman: a woman with shortcomings, a person or object that was presumed lost shows up again

30. Lily: lack of guidance or fatherly support, missing out on a promotion

31. Sun: a shortage or a theft comes to light, impaired vision

32. Moon: theft at the work place, missing his work, work that supplements shortages, a pawnbroker

33. Key: do not continue before the shortcomings are detected and supplemented

34. Fish: a sensational theft, having no vision or self-awareness

35. Anchor: missing or losing your true love

36. Cross: a chronic shortage, insufficient discipline, responsibility, perseverance or patience

24
HEART

Keywords: being in love, love, art and beauty, lust for life

SIGNIFICANCE OF THE CARD COMBINATIONS

1. **Rider:** a conversation about love
2. **Clover:** creativity will be flowing
3. **Ship:** an investment in (works of) art
4. **House:** a beautiful dwelling, a man in love
5. **Tree:** matters of the heart or an unhealthy infatuation
6. **Clouds:** feelings of love are turned down
7. **Snake:** the infatuation is an illusion
8. **Coffin:** a compulsive or abrupt and unpleasant ending love
9. **Bouquet:** a satisfactory, happy time, holiday
10. **Scythe:** a budding love will not end happily
11. **Whip:** sexuality, love
12. **Birds:** a heartache will not last for long
13. **Child:** a spontaneous infatuation, loving children
14. **Fox:** distrust in affairs of the heart
15. **Bear:** jealousy and love go hand in hand
16. **Stars:** a new infatuation
17. **Stork:** feelings of love are subject to change
18. **Dog:** a deep infatuation, a friend is an artist
19. **Tower:** building a wall, not allowing or not showing feelings of love
20. **Garden:** artistic circles, tolerant friends, falling in love with a friend
21. **Mountain:** heartbreak
22. **Way:** a choice from the heart, regrets about a metaphysical issue, doubts about a work of art
23. **Mice:** losing a love, missing love
25. **Ring:** a romance, art trade
26. **Book:** a secret, unspoken love or infatuation
27. **Letter:** a love letter
28. **Man:** a lovable, charming man, a man in love
29. **Woman:** a lovable, charming woman, a woman in love
30. **Lily:** love and friendship go together
31. **Sun:** being in love brings joy and mental strength
32. **Moon:** working in the artistic or creative sector, a business dinner, a business trip
33. **Key:** follow your heart, look at things from a different angle, be tolerant
34. **Fish:** many passionate infatuations, big or major works of art
35. **Anchor:** the infatuation in this romance is not fading
36. **Cross:** the infatuation is cooling off, suppressed feelings of love, a lack of creative inspiration

25
RING

Keywords: relationships, cooperation, teamwork, a merger, going hand in hand

SIGNIFICANCE OF THE CARD COMBINATIONS

1. Rider: a conversation with the spouse or partner
2. Clover: a troublesome relation will be restored
3. Ship: a relationship based on finances
4. House: a happy marriage in which you feel safe
5. Tree: a troublesome relationship
6. Clouds: difficulties in a relationship, blockades
7. Snake: dishonesty in the relationship
8. Coffin: an unhappy or compulsive relationship or a relationship that is about to end
9. Bouquet: a peaceful relationship
10. Scythe: a temporary break in a relationship
11. Whip: a trial of strength within a relationship
12. Birds: a good and stable relationship, temporary problems in a relationship
13. Child: an honest and open relationship
14. Fox: distrust, ruse and deceit in a relationship

15. Bear: discord and irritation within a relationship
16. Stars: a successful or new partnership
17. Stork: a change within a relationship or partnership
18. Dog: a reliable relationship
19. Tower: an emotionally distant relationship, an official relationship, a corporate merger
20. Garden: a good partnership, collaboration, a close and harmonious marriage
21. Mountain: grief over a relationship
22. Way: facing a choice regarding a relationship
23. Mice: missing a relationship, a diminishing relationship
24. Heart: a romance
26. Book: learning how to handle relationships, this relationship has many secrets
27. Letter: receiving a message from a partner, a message indicating collaboration
28. Man: this man is willing to start a relationship
29. Woman: this woman is willing to start a relationship

30. Lily: a platonic relationship, this relationship is based on support and shelter
31. Sun: 'spring is in the air' in this relationship, a cause for celebration
32. Moon: a business-connection, a partnership or a merger, a matchmaking agency
33. Key: collaborate, do not continue on your own, a successful relationship
34. Fish: multiple relationships, expansion within the relationship
35. Anchor: a close and harmonious romance
36. Cross: the end of an old relationship and the beginning of a new one, a relationship out of a sense of duty

26
BOOK

Keywords: secrecy, missing information, keeping silent about something, education

SIGNIFICANCE OF THE CARD COMBINATIONS

1. Rider: not everything has been said or understood

2. Clover: the urge to unravel secrets

3. Ship: school fees, tuition costs, secrecy regarding finances

4. House: at home not everything is said, secrets regarding a house or dwelling

5. Tree: an unknown illness or not anticipating an illness

6. Clouds: hushed-up problems

7. Snake: 'a little white lie...'

8. Coffin: a taboo, not wanting to face something

9. Bouquet: literature for leisure

10. Scythe: unconscious or unspoken fears

11. Whip: secret plans, secrets of sexual nature

12. Birds: a misunderstanding due to a lack of knowledge or because of holding out on something

13. Child: the child is doing homework, is at school or keeps a secret

14. Fox: a secret strategy

15. Bear: unspoken unease and irritation, an unsatisfying education

16. Stars: a purposeful study, research yield results

17. Stork: keeping a change obscured

18. Dog: a college friend, a friend with a secret or a secret friendship

19. Tower: an educational or research institute, a publishing company, an (academic) education

20. Garden: friendly and helpful study partners, a secret society

21. Mountain: learning problems, problems at school, an educational institution is not helpful

22. Way: not being able to choose regarding a school or education, doubting the aim

23. Mice: a lack of education or knowledge, an educational institution falls short, an undiscovered or unexplained theft

24. Heart: a secret, unspoken love or infatuation

25. Ring: learning how to handle relationships, this relationship has many secrets

27. Letter: an announcement in secret, the diagnosis is kept silent

28. Man: a mysterious or studious man

29. Woman: a mysterious or studious woman

30. Lily: a (study) coach or a (study) guide

31. Sun: clarification, a revealing or educational book

32. Moon: the book business, education, a vocational education, research

33. Key: acquire knowledge by reading a lot of books or by getting an education

34. Fish: a big secret, secret sciences, books as the basis of knowledge, a vision

35. Anchor: a secret and unspoken love, a bookworm

36. Cross: keeping silent about something out of shame or insecurity, disciplinary studying or research

27
LETTER

Keywords: news, a message, documents, a decision or conclusion, a diagnosis

SIGNIFICANCE OF THE CARD COMBINATIONS

1. Rider: a decision is announced

2. Clover: news arrives that brings improvement

3. Ship: a message about money, a bank statement

4. House: a message about a house or from home

5. Tree: diagnosis of a disease

6. Clouds: an unpleasant or refused message

7. Snake: fake news, mail is delivered to the wrong address

8. Coffin: a threatening letter

9. Bouquet: a gift by mail

10. Scythe: an unpleasant message or a warning by mail

11. Whip: an angry letter, a rash decision; e-mail, the internet

12. Birds: a diagnosis based on misunderstandings, an unpleasant message bringing beneficial changes

13. Child: mail from a child, exchange of letters regarding a child

14. Fox: this letter is meant to lead you astray

15. Bear: a decision made out of discord and irritation

16. Stars: very good news by mail, a promising decision

17. Stork: a vague decision, keeping all options open

18. Dog: mail from a friend

19. Tower: an official letter or document

20. Garden: exchanging messages with friends

21. Mountain: a letter containing an unpleasant message, a sad decision

22. Way: a message is already on the way, a message involves a choice

23. Mice: a letter gets lost, lost papers, message about a theft

24. Heart: a love letter

25. Ring: receiving a message from a partner, a message indicating collaboration

26. Book: an announcement in secret, the diagnosis is kept silent

28. Man: a decisive man

29. Woman: a decisive woman

30. Lily: making a decision to move up, receiving a message about a promotion

31. Sun: a clarifying or joyful message, the decision is obvious and clear

32. Moon: a message about work, a decision regarding work or work-related activities

33. Key: this message brings the right solution, determining the right diagnosis, cut the knot

34. Fish: a message with a vision, receiving a lot of mail, positive messages

35. Anchor: a love letter, choosing for a 'true love'

36. Cross: a message regarding adversity, sluggish coverage, little mail or mail that was received too late

28
MAN

Keywords: the 'personal card' when the questioner is male or the partner of a female questioner

SIGNIFICANCE OF THE CARD COMBINATIONS

1. Rider: for a man: someone wants to get in touch with you; for a woman: conversations with the partner

2. Clover: this man is honest and trustworthy

3. Ship: a wealthy man, a travelling man, a foreign man

4. House: a protective, paternal man

5. Tree: a sick man

6. Clouds: a man in trouble

7. Snake: a dishonest man, focused on appearances

8. Coffin: a powerful man, a man in a process of transformation

9. Bouquet: a quiet man, this man receives a gift

10. Scythe: an insecure or inexperienced man

11. Whip: an energetic, assertive man, or an angry man

12. Birds: brief suffering for the man

13. Child: a man with a child, a frank, spontaneous man

14. Fox: a distrusting man, a cunning tactic

15. Bear: a dissatisfied or jealous man

16. Stars: a strong-willed, successful man

17. Stork: a man who constantly changes plans or aims, a man in an alternating situation

18. Dog: this man is standing by his friend's side

19. Tower: this man is hiding behind a self-built imaginary wall

20. Garden: this man has a large circle of friends and is very sociable

21. Mountain: a sad, brooding man, a negative man

22. Way: this man is having second thoughts and finds it hard to choose, he is on the road a lot

23. Mice: a man with shortcomings, a person or object that was presumed lost shows up again

24. Heart: a lovable, charming man, a man in love

25. Ring: this man is willing to start a relationship

26. Book: a mysterious or studious man

27. Letter: a decisive man

29. Woman: these two make a great couple, good contact between partners or friends

30. Lily: an older man, a helpful man, a man getting a promotion

31. Sun: a cheerful, energetic man

32. Moon: this man is extremely occupied with his work

33. Key: this man has the situation under control, the man can solve problems or other issues

34. Fish: this man is convinced of himself, his opinion and ideas

35. Anchor: this man loves someone very much

36. Cross: this man is momentarily experiencing (a lot of) adversity

29
WOMAN

Keywords:
the 'personal card' when the questioner is female or the partner of a male questioner

SIGNIFICANCE OF THE CARD COMBINATIONS

1. Rider: conversations with the female partner; for a woman: someone wants to get in touch with you

2. Clover: this woman is honest and trustworthy

3. Ship: a wealthy woman, a travelling woman, a foreign woman

4. House: a caring, domestic woman

5. Tree: a sick woman

6. Clouds: a woman in trouble

7. Snake: a dishonest woman, focused on appearances

8. Coffin: a powerful woman, a woman in a process of transformation

9. Bouquet: a quiet woman, this woman receives a gift

10. Scythe: an insecure or inexperienced woman

11. Whip: an energetic, assertive woman, an angry woman

12. Birds: brief suffering for the woman

13. Child: a woman with a child, a frank, spontaneous woman

14. Fox: a distrusting woman, a cunning tactic

15. Bear: a dissatisfied or jealous woman

16. Stars: a strong-willed, successful woman

17. Stork: a woman who constantly changes plans or goals, a woman in a changeable situation

18. Dog: this woman is standing by her friend's side

19. Tower: a woman is hiding behind a self-built imaginary wall

20. Garden: this woman has a large circle of friends and is very sociable

21. Mountain: a sad brooding woman

22. Way: this woman is having second thoughts and finds it hard to choose, she is on the road a lot

23. Mice: a woman with shortcomings, a person or object that was presumed lost shows up again

24. Heart: a lovable, charming woman, a woman in love

25. Ring: this woman is willing to start a relationship

26. Book: a mysterious or studious woman

27. Letter: a decisive woman

28. Man: these two make a great couple, good contact between partners or friends

30. Lily: an older woman, a helpful woman, a woman getting a promotion

31. Sun: a cheerful, energetic woman

32. Moon: this woman is extremely occupied with her work

33. Key: this woman has the situation under control, this woman can solve problems and other issues

34. Fish: this woman is convinced of herself, her opinions and ideas

35. Anchor: this woman loves someone very much

36. Cross: this woman is momentarily experiencing (a lot of) adversity

30
LILY

Keywords:
a coach, a 'patron' or 'patroness', a benefactor, promotion, old age

SIGNIFICANCE OF THE CARD COMBINATIONS

1. Rider: news from a friend or coach, a conversation about a promotion

2. Clover: a promotion (at work) might be expected

3. Ship: a raise due to promotion, coaching costs, retirement

4. House: a paternal 'patron', getting ahead thanks to the father

5. Tree: an unjust promotion

6. Clouds: problems with a promotion or with aging

7. Snake: an unfair promotion, a dishonest coach

8. Coffin: a powerful or manipulative 'patron'

9. Bouquet: a promotion, this coach does nothing helpful

10. Scythe: a promotion is at risk, an inexperienced coach

11. Whip: aspiring to get bigger and better, pursuing a promotion

12. Birds: career problems quickly solve themselves

13. Child: a child is protected, a wise child

14. Fox: an unreliable coach

15. Bear: dissatisfactory guidance, displeasure with a career

16. Stars: a promotion, purposeful guidance

17. Stork: a change of career, help when making a change

18. Dog: this 'patron' is also a reliable friend

19. Tower: having a so-called high placed benefactor

20. Garden: moving up the ladder through networking, having the support of a good friend

21. Mountain: career problems, struggling with ageing

22. Way: a choice to get a promotion, the coach's choice

23. Mice: lack of guidance or fatherly support, missing out on a promotion

24. Heart: love and friendship go together

25. Ring: a platonic relationship, this relationship is based on support and shelter

26. Book: a (study) coach or a (study) guide

27. Letter: making a decision to move up, receiving a message about a promotion

28. Man: an older man, a helpful man, a man getting a promotion

29. Woman: an older woman, a helpful woman, a woman getting a promotion

31. Sun: a visionary coach, a wise older person, happiness in a career

32. Moon: a promotion, help and guidance at work, career guidance, working with the elderly

33. Key: a coach or 'patron' can resolve the issue

34. Fish: a (self-proclaimed) guru, there is no arguing with this coach

35. Anchor: love in later life, the coach offers help and support, a platonic love

36. Cross: a career encounters opposition and delay, a career phase has been closed

31
SUN

Keywords: happiness, optimism, light, charisma, self-confidence, guidance

SIGNIFICANCE OF THE CARD COMBINATIONS

1. Rider: positive news, positive thoughts
2. Clover: thanks to better understanding great times are approaching
3. Ship: an excellent financial situation, travelling to someplace warm
4. House: a sunny house, a happy father, luck in regard to housing
5. Tree: insight about a disease, an eye disease
6. Clouds: gaining insight in a problem, a civil servant is verifying an issue
7. Snake: a lie comes to light or an illusion proves to be a disillusion
8. Coffin: possessing great transformative powers, shamanism
9. Bouquet: being quiet provides perception, a sunny, cheerful holiday, a nice gift
10. Scythe: fear comes to light and is overcome, youthful recklessness
11. Whip: a very big ego, great physical strength and virility, self-centeredness
12. Birds: inspiration, perception, intuition, clairvoyance
13. Child: a light-hearted and cheerful child, a happy childhood

14. Fox: an unknown opponent is exposed
15. Bear: not granting yourself or others a good reputation, not being allowed to be yourself
16. Stars: unexpected success, having a clear target in mind
17. Stork: a beneficial change
18. Dog: lasting happiness, a happy and inspiring friendship
19. Tower: being able to perceive 'dividing walls', screening a business
20. Garden: a happy time with social contacts, understanding on the social front, popularity
21. Mountain: unexpected opposition, an unexpected opponent, mood-swings, a silver lining
22. Way: an outing with lovely weather, a clear choice, tolerance in traffic
23. Mice: a shortage or a theft comes to light, impaired vision
24. Heart: being in love brings joy and mental strength
25. Ring: 'spring is in the air' in this relationship, a cause for celebration

26. Book: clarification, a revealing or educational book
27. Letter: a clarifying or joyful message, the decision is obvious and clear
28. Man: a cheerful, energetic man
29. Woman: a cheerful, energetic woman
30. Lily: a visionary coach, a wise older person, happiness in a career
32. Moon: insights regarding work (activities), yoga and meditation, the 'unseen world', spirituality
33. Key: surround yourself with (sun)light and warmth, be positive and optimistic
34. Fish: a clarifying vision, successful expansion, a great success
35. Anchor: a happy love, optimism as a lifeline
36. Cross: understanding of one's own limitations, self-analysis, not being discouraged by adversity

32 MOON

Keywords: employment and occupation, career, success in social challenges, emotion

SIGNIFICANCE OF THE CARD COMBINATIONS

1. Rider: staff meetings, work related to communication or (a) language, work-related news

2. Clover: improving working conditions, agreement, (marriage) proposal

3. Ship: earnings from activities (abroad), working in the tourist industry or with ships

4. House: working at home, real estate

5. Tree: the work situation is awkward, unhealthy work, working in health care, mistakes at work

6. Clouds: problems at work, no revenues from work

7. Snake: returning to old (bad) habits, a profession in science (chemistry)

8. Coffin: work comes to an end, work to do with death, a to heavy workload, reorganisation at work

9. Bouquet: temporarily less work; voluntary work, professional help

10. Scythe: a student, no work experience, a dangerous profession, work is in danger

11. Whip: quarrels at work, working hard, pulling out all the stops

12. Birds: a professional nurse, brief difficulties at work

13. Child: working with children at school or in youth care

14. Fox: corporate espionage, career through ruse and tactics, gossip and deceit at work

15. Bear: envy, irritations and dissatisfaction at the workplace

16. Stars: success or a new promising goal at work

17. Stork: changes at work, a flexible job, a job agency

18. Dog: a reliable employee, friendship at work, working with animals

19. Tower: making a career for yourself, ambition, a job high up

20. Garden: working (together) with people, clubs and societies, 'networking', a public appearance

21. Mountain: competition and contradictions at work, worrying about work

22. Way: a choice regarding work or profession, road works, working outside, transport industry

23. Mice: theft at the work place, missing his work, work that supplements shortages, a pawnbroker

24. Heart: working in the artistic or creative sector, a business dinner, a business trip

25. Ring: a business-connection, a partnership or a merger, a matchmaking agency

26. Book: the book business, education, a vocational education, research

27. Letter: a message about work, a decision regarding work or work-related activities

28. Man: this man is extremely occupied with his work

29. Woman: this woman is extremely occupied with her work

30. Lily: promotion, help and guidance at work, career guidance, working with the elderly

31. Sun: insights regarding work (activities), yoga and meditation, the 'unseen world', spirituality

33. Key: advice, success and possibilities regarding work (activities), a therapist

34. Fish: expansion of work activities, a business expansion, stock going up, public relations, advertising

35. Anchor: competence, love for the job, a serious relationship

36. Cross: less work, workload, work pressure, frustrating work, a delay at work

33
KEY

Keywords:
the solution, advice, possibilities, succeeding, success, therapy, doing the right thing

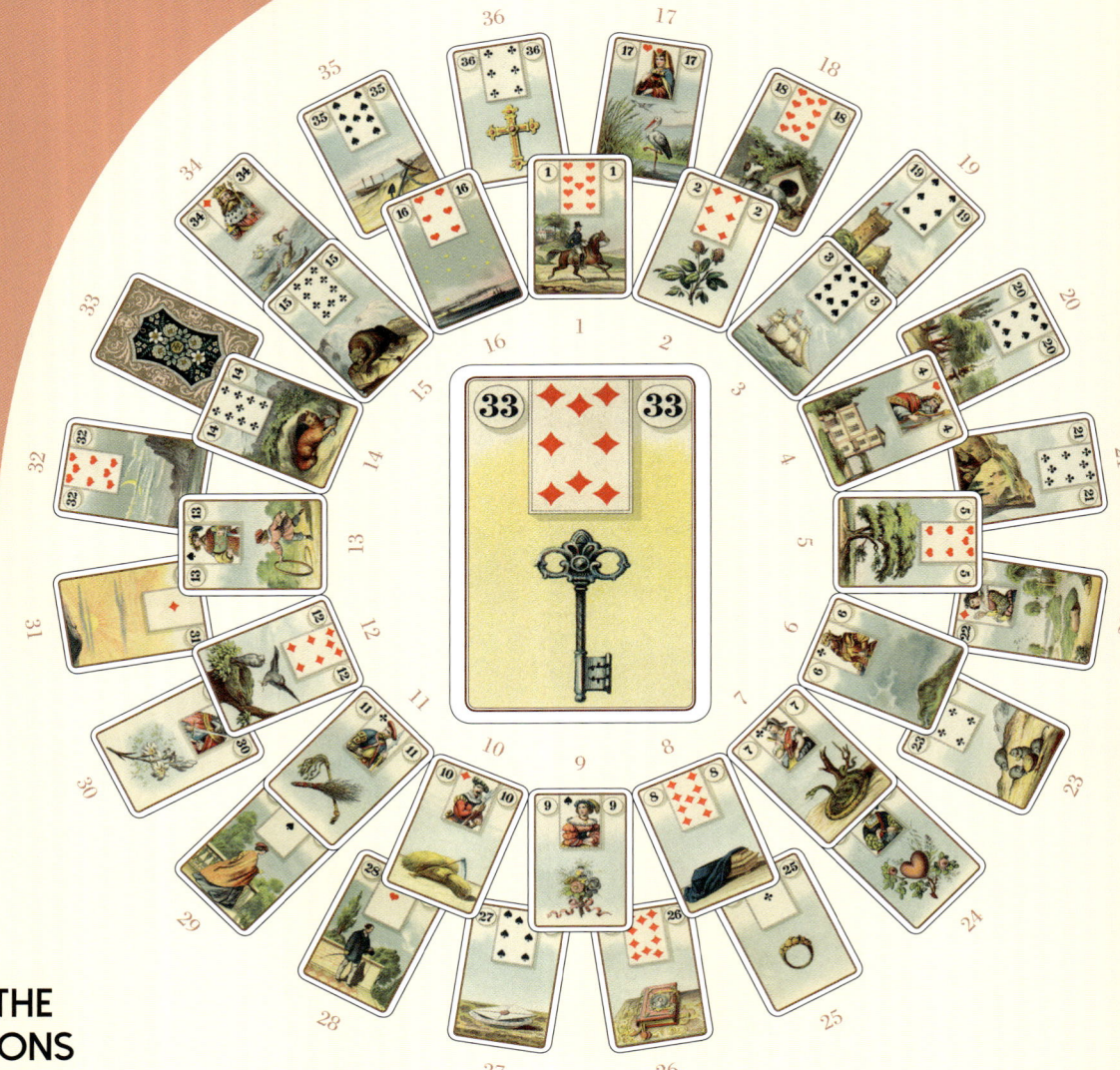

SIGNIFICANCE OF THE CARD COMBINATIONS

1. Rider: receiving a solution, a successful or a therapeutic conversation

2. Clover: the fulfilment of a wish becomes a possibility

3. Ship: solving problems with financial means

4. House: advice to stay at home, the personal situation is under control

5. Tree: therapy and advice to take better care of your health

6. Clouds: a problem is obstructing progress, but can be solved

7. Snake: pay more attention to your looks, fantasy offers a solution

8. Coffin: accepting a loss, a successful surgery

9. Bouquet: the solution is... doing nothing

10. Scythe: fear or danger can be resolved or eliminated

11. Whip: the solution is undertaking resolute action

12. Birds: resolving a misunderstanding, the need to take care of someone

13. Child: learning from a child, advice to be open and spontaneous

14. Fox: the advice not to be too trusting

15. Bear: the advice to become aware of your own irritations and unease

16. Stars: the advice to act purposefully and determined creates success

17. Stork: the advice to adjust or to make a change

18. Dog: the advice to spend more time with friends, a friend provides the solution

19. Tower: a separation or divorce

20. Garden: give more attention to social contacts, a circle of acquaintances provides solution, group therapy

21. Mountain: recognising one's own grief, protect yourself against other people's quarrels

22. Way: postponing a decision in order to investigate its possibilities and consequences

23. Mice: do not continue before the shortcomings are detected and supplemented

24. Heart: follow your heart, look at things from a different angle, be tolerant

25. Ring: collaborate, do not continue on your own, a successful relationship

26. Book: acquire knowledge by reading a lot of books or by getting an education

27. Letter: this message brings the right solution, determining the right diagnosis, cut the knot

28. Man: this man has the situation under control, the man can solve problems or other issues

29. Woman: this woman has the situation under control, this woman can solve problems and other issues

30. Lily: a coach or the right therapy can solve the issue

31. Sun: surround yourself with (sun)light and warmth, be positive and optimistic

32. Moon: advice, success and possibilities regarding work (activities), a therapist

34. Fish: the advice to broaden the view, to think big, water therapy

35. Anchor: the advice to seek something to hold on to, a 'true love'

36. Cross: structure in life, accomplishing the mission with patience, discipline and perseverance

34

FISH

Keywords: expansion, increase, riches, success, wealth, vision, self-awareness

SIGNIFICANCE OF THE CARD COMBINATIONS

1. Rider: increase of contacts, constant phone calls, good news

2. Clover: the desire for ever more and better

3. Ship: a lot of money, foreign currencies, traveling

4. House: a big house, a villa or mansion, possibly a hotel

5. Tree: the water management is defunct, wishing too much, an unhealthy view on life in general

6. Clouds: believing in difficulties, problems with (believing) religion, no confidence in faith

7. Snake: unfulfilled desires, a materialistic attitude to life

8. Coffin: forcing your opinion on others, exaggerated sense of self-consciousness, intimidation

9. Bouquet: a rise comes naturally, a great gift

10. Scythe: fear of thinking 'big' about yourself, negative self-image, fears regarding religion or faith

11. Whip: great enthusiasm and self-confidence, heroism

12. Birds: the concept of life or self-awareness leads to temporary problems

13. Child: many children, having a naïve outlook on life

14. Fox: a secret opponent is convincingly spreading gossip

15. Bear: discord due to a negative approach on life in general

16. Stars: a huge hit, but also: too much willpower and excessive self-awareness

17. Stork: confidently following the 'flow of life', a change for the better

18. Dog: having a large circle of friends, friends with the same vision

19. Tower: expressing an official point of view, a multinational, the ministry

20. Garden: expansion of a circle of friends and acquaintances

21. Mountain: frustrated ambitions, meeting a lot of resistance

22. Way: having a lot of options, a generous offer, waterways

23. Mice: a sensational theft, having no vision or self-awareness

24. Heart: many passionate infatuations, big or major works of art

25. Ring: multiple relationships, expansion within the relationship

26. Book: a big secret, secret sciences, books as the basis of knowledge, a vision

27. Letter: a message with a vision, receiving a lot of mail, positive messages

28. Man: this man is convinced of himself, his opinion and ideas

29. Woman: this woman is convinced of herself, her opinions and ideas

30. Lily: a (self-proclaimed) guru, there is no arguing with this coach

31. Sun: a clarifying vision, successful expansion, great success

32. Moon: expansion of work activities, a business expansion, stock going up, public relations, advertising

33. Key: the advice to broaden the view, to think big, water therapy

35. Anchor: love for life, a religious love

36. Cross: extremes, ups and downs, religious frustration, a narrow view

35
ANCHOR

Keywords: true love, talent, help and support, stability, fortunate in business

SIGNIFICANCE OF THE CARD COMBINATIONS

1. **Rider:** a declaration of love
2. **Clover:** romantic grievances are solved
3. **Ship:** materialism, love for money and possessions, a good trip
4. **House:** a safe 'home port'
5. **Tree:** an unhealthy love, clinging to the wrong person or situation
6. **Clouds:** a problematic love, refraining from feelings of love
7. **Snake:** leaning and relying on illusions
8. **Coffin:** a compulsive love
9. **Bouquet:** a calm, stable love
10. **Scythe:** insecurity about love
11. **Whip:** a strong sexual, true love
12. **Birds:** a brief heartache
13. **Child:** deep love for the child, the child loves you, a spontaneous love
14. **Fox:** not being able to trust love as well as the the current relationship
15. **Bear:** in this relationship is a lot of jealousy
16. **Stars:** a new love comes into view, a good cause

17. **Stork:** the romance still exists, but is subject to heavy fluctuations
18. **Dog:** a loyal romance
19. **Tower:** not yielding to true love, giving all attention to a professional life
20. **Garden:** loving each other deeply and enjoying spending time in each other's presence
21. **Mountain:** a painful heartbreak over a true love
22. **Way:** a true love necessitates an important choice
23. **Mice:** missing or losing your true love
24. **Heart:** the infatuation in this romance is not fading
25. **Ring:** a close and harmonious romance
26. **Book:** a secret and unspoken love, a bookworm
27. **Letter:** a love letter, choosing for a 'true love'
28. **Man:** this man loves someone very much
29. **Woman:** this woman loves someone very much
30. **Lily:** love in later life, the coach offers help and support, a platonic love

31. **Sun:** a happy love, optimism as lifeline
32. **Moon:** love for the job, a serious relationship, competence
33. **Key:** the advice to seek something to hold on to, a 'true love'
34. **Fish:** a love for life, religious love
36. **Cross:** feelings of love diminishing, an unexpected encounter may be a new love...

36
CROSS

Keywords: decrease, sobriety, discipline, natural cycles, delay, opposition, gloominess

SIGNIFICANCE OF THE CARD COMBINATIONS

1. Rider: news or a conversation about hindrance

2. Clover: improvement is approaching, but slowly...

3. Ship: financial losses, a financial setback, a trip falls short

4. House: a house that is too small or sad, an old building in bad shape

5. Tree: disorders of the bones or teeth, a chronic disease, sclerosis

6. Clouds: a structural problem

7. Snake: disorders of the bones, toothache, unable to keep business rolling

8. Coffin: excessive self-discipline, the end of an era

9. Bouquet: forced rest, following the middle way

10. Scythe: misery causes fear and insecurity

11. Whip: limited energy, restrained anger

12. Birds: structural misunderstandings

13. Child: a child is depressed, a setback involving children

14. Fox: mistrust arises from frustration and insecurity

15. Bear: irritation and unease originate from self-imposed restrictions

16. Stars: keep calm, don't skip one step on the stairs to success

17. Stork: a change comes with adversity and delay

18. Dog: (care giving) obligations towards friends

19. Tower: a hard time for business, obligations towards the authorities

20. Garden: the circle of friends and acquaintances is getting smaller

21. Mountain: long lasting or suppressed grief

22. Way: a new phase of life entails limited options

23. Mice: a chronic shortage, insufficient discipline, responsibility, perseverance or patience

24. Heart: the infatuation is cooling off, suppressed feelings of love, a lack of creative inspiration

25. Ring: the end of an old relationship and the beginning of a new one, a relationship out of a sense of duty

26. Book: keeping silent about something out of shame or insecurity, disciplinary studying or research

27. Letter: a message regarding adversity, sluggish coverage, little mail or mail that was received too late

28. Man: this man is momentarily experiencing (a lot of) adversity

29. Woman: this woman is momentarily experiencing (a lot of) adversity

30. Lily: a career encounters opposition and delay, a career phase has been closed

31. Sun: understanding of one's own limitations, self-analysis, not being discouraged by adversity

32. Moon: less work, workload, work pressure, frustrating work, a delay at work

33. Key: structure in life, accomplishing the mission with patience, discipline and perseverance

34. Fish: extremes, ups and downs, religious frustration, a narrow view

35. Anchor: feelings of love diminishing, an unexpected encounter may be a new love...

LE GRAND TABLEAU
THE BIG SPREAD

METHOD WITH ALL 36 CARDS

This spread uses all 36 cards. With the by now acquired knowledge of the card combinations through 'connective thinking', this spread can be interpreted in-depth and in detail. The spread offers an overall picture of the cards and consists of four rows of eight cards each. The remaining four cards make up a fifth row, centred at the bottom.

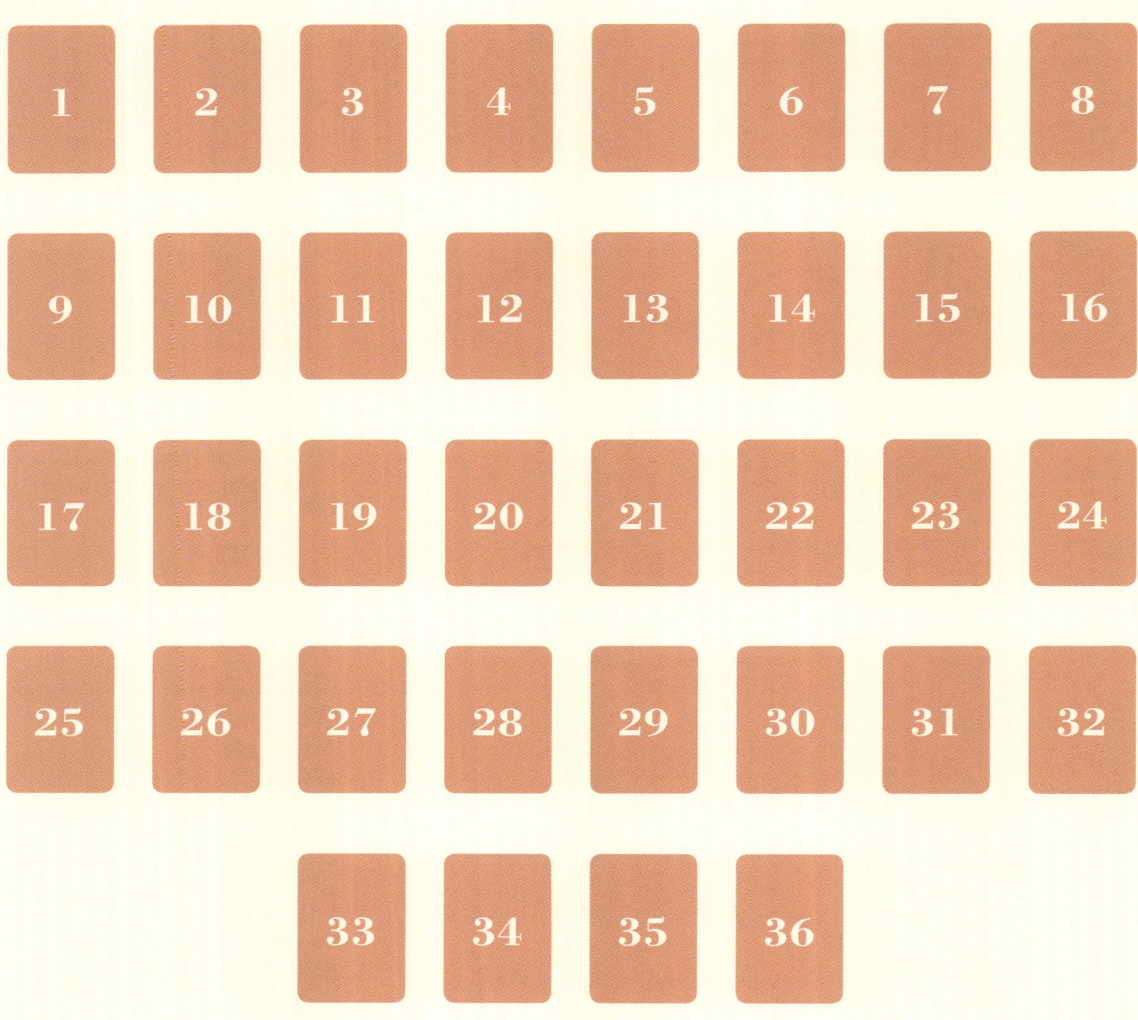

- Check where the card representing the *questioner*, your own *personal card*, is located (resp. the *Man* or the *Woman*): at the top, in the middle or at the bottom of the spread? This is a first indication of how much control you have over your life. Now look at the cards surrounding your *personal card*. These cards are the most influential. Whatever lies below the *personal card* (*Man* or *Woman*), we can handle.

- Check which cards are located next to your *personal card* and pay attention which way your personal card *points*. Cards that are located *above* the personal card might point to a situation that is out of control.

- Check the position of the *Coffin*. For instance: you are going through a period of transformation, maybe even a crisis. If the *Coffin* is located under your *personal card*, you might have some influence on the process. The process is probably coming to an end and certain things are already clear. If the *Coffin* resides *above your personal card*, you have no control over the process, it is probably still at an early stage. The neighbouring cards determine the nature of the transformation and its progress. Positive cards lighten this process - the *Sun* for example does so literally as well as figuratively. But if the *Moon* is near, you need to be aware of black magic, the end of a job and/or a strong outburst of emotions.

- Explore which other *personal cards* are located near your own *personal card*.

- The position of the *Lily* is of importance: is this card situated under your own *personal card*, you are doing inadmissible things. If the *Lily* resides under other cards, then that is happening in another area of our life. The cards above the *Lily* will give us more information.

- Check if the *Ring* is located to the left or to the right of *(y)our personal card*. If the *Ring* is situated on the right side, that indicates a relationship. Check where the partner is located. Is it unclear whether or not a relationship might be expected, then the partner card points to the possible future partner. When the partner card and the *Ring* are not in the neighbourhood of your *personal card*, the relationship will take some time to show itself.

- Now look for the *answers* you seek. If, for instance, you want information about your work situation, check where the *Moon* is located. If it is far away, this situation is not on the agenda for now, or not important.

- The financial situation is represented by the *Ship* and the *Fish*.

- The *Ship* provides information about traveling and foreign countries.

- For written messages, documents and contracts, look at the *Letter*. For verbal announcements, pay attention to the *Rider*.

- The *Child* gives information about a child. If there are more children, look for their respective *personal cards*.

- For questions regarding social life, look at the *Dog* and the *Garden*.

- For health issues, look at the *Tree*. If the *Tree* is not positioned close to your own *personal card*, you don't have to worry for anything unpleasant.

- Looking for solutions: check the location of the *Key* and its surrounding cards. If the *Key* is situated near the *personal card*, issues can be resolved by ourselves.

Connective thinking… In learning to understand the meaning of the cards, it is important to interpret the cards according to their location in the spread: close by the *personal card*, above it (or else) and in relation with all other cards. That way, you learn effortlessly the relevant associations between the cards and furthermore, you will discover you own personal card combinations. Check the notes on your earlier spreads regularly, they will prove to be a big help.

THE ADVANTAGES OF THE BIG SPREAD (LE GRAND TABLEAU)

It might occur that the complexity of your questions makes the interpretation of the cards seem virtually impossible. For instance, you want to gain insight in the functioning of the company you work for because you are looking for a new job, but is has several branches and departments. A complex structure that makes it quite difficult to see the overall picture. And above that, you have already three job offers!

Or, at another level, you are searching for a new school for your child, but the options are endless. There are too many schools to choose from. And then, then there is only one card available representing work or education! At first sight, The Big Spread seems unsuitable, almost unworkable. Thankfully that is not the case. The example hereafter shows how to get answers to such complex questions.

Example

Starting point is a company that has six divisions. Pick up the cards and remove the *Man* and the *Woman*. Afterwards you wash (shuffle) the cards like you always do. On a piece of paper, you write down the six divisions of the company one after the other. Now you pick one card per division and put their names right behind the company structure:

1. Management: 31. the Sun

2. Administration: 23. the Mice

3. Distribution: 8. the Coffin

4. Production A: 34. the Fish

5. Production B: 36. the Cross

6. Sales: 9. the Bouquet

As you can see, these cards already offer a fair outline of the functioning of the divisions.

Management is self-confident and has in all probability insight in the company. The surrounding cards however will have to confirm this later on.

Administration has a problem, for example a poor functioning of the staff or equipment, but theft is also a possibility. This will be determined later on by the surrounding cards.

Distribution is in a phase of complete reorganisation. The neighbouring cards will give a more definite answer about its further progress.

Production A is on their way up, production is increasing. This was also the reason for the required reorganisation in the distribution division.

Production B has a decreasing producing. Whether this is only temporary or not, will be shown by the surrounding cards.

The **Sales** division can be either passive or is functioning satisfactorily. This too is something the surrounding cards will have to show.

Now you have an idea which divisions need your attention. Return all the cards, including the *Man* and the *Woman* to the deck and wash (shuffle) all the cards again. Subsequently, you can start with **The Big Spread**, because since you now know where to find the respective divisions, you can start interpreting the cards.

The neighbouring cards might show that the *Sun* combined with the *Management* shows that they are proud, vain and ambitious, and use the 'sunny energy' to increase their own status instead of the proper functioning of the company. This may be confirmed when the *Sun* card is located above and away from the cards that symbolise the other divisions.

The *Sales* division has the *Bouquet* and the *Cross*. That could mean that this division is stuck in routine: the *Bouquet*, passivity; the *Cross*, being stuck in old ways, on autopilot. This division is possibly not very dynamic and does not adapt to the increased production of **Division A**. As result not enough material is purchased causing a slow production.

When you learn how to 'play' with the basic significance of the cards and reflect on what the cards may represent, the interpretation becomes ever more vivid. However, reading and interpreting the cards is and will remain always personal. You're a free in determining which card represents a certain quality or situation. For instance, ask yourself how a recession would be represented (in a spread). In all probability, the *Cross* would occur. When you choose the combination of the *Cross* and the *Fish*, to you this combination will indicate a recession. Also, you are free to decide that the *Dog* represents your favourite horse. Or, that, in your perception, the combination of the *Moon* and the *Sun* represents white magic. Then, to you, that is their relevant meaning. Or you are a politician and to you the card combination of the *Cross* and the *Sun* represent the authorities, and the *Garden* represents your political party. If that is how it you experience the cards, excellent: then that is how it is going to be.

PRACTICE SHEET
QUIZ YOURSELF, TEST YOUR KNOWLEDGE!

Place one Lenormand card at the centre and write down everything you know about this card!
And, what do you know about this card in combination with the other Lenormand cards?

CARD NAME:

SIGNIFICANCE OF THE CARD:

CARD COMBINATION:

NOTES ON THE PRACTICE SHEET

NOTES ON THE PRACTICE SHEET